Poetry Un-Chained
Memoirs of the Unhanged

Timjae A. D'allo

POETRY UN-CHANIED

Maybe purchased for education, business or sales promotional use.

For information, please contact:

Stephani Richardson

Stephrich09@gmail.com

Cover Design: Stephani Richardson

Editor: Stephani Richardson

ISBN: 0-9840456-9-4
ISBN-13: 978-0-9840456-9-3

Library of Congress Cataloging – in – Publication data:

Printed in the United States of America

DEDICATION

I dedicate this book of passionate expression and pain, to my wife and children all of who I feel safe in venting my frustrations about the world to most. And to Allah, who keeps me set upon the straight path.

Contents

ACKNOWLEDGMENTS

Recognizing my wife Stephani is both an honor and a reward, for being a pillar of strength in my weakness, and a beacon of light in my darkness, I remain forever indebted to you. To my children Timmyanni and Tim Jr. I owe my very existence, because you both are my reason for living. To my mother Yvonne, for constantly being a solid foundation in my life when I am most unsteady. As well, I must acknowledge a very good friend along my journey that has been an inspiration to this creation, Vincent Sherrill, for our early morning battle conscious sessions "Asante"!" And lastly, but most important in the success of this book, I would like to recognize the fallen, the assassinated, and the families of the aforementioned stolen lineage – black people.

And a special thanks to Award winning Author Le'Taxione™ for his professional advice and editorial prowess. I truly appreciate your assistance and support, your vision and most of all your spiritual tutelage.

Al hamdu lil lahi

(All praise is for Allah)

Poetry Un-Chained
Memoirs of the Unhanged

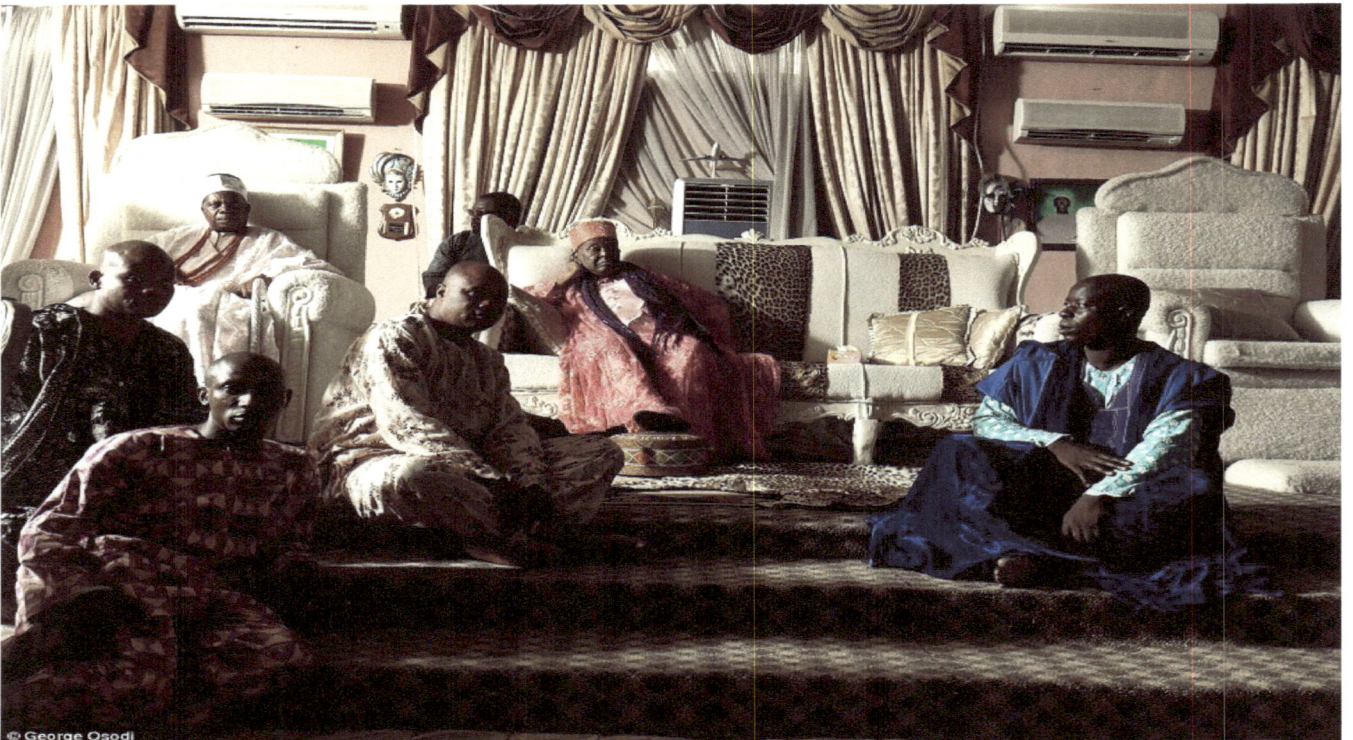

© George Osodi

NEXT LIFETIME

Sometimes I wonder; who might I be?

Ancestrally; If not for slavery.

Would I exist; with a rich name of significance

And grow strong in a village, filled with love and togetherness?

Or if my ancestry were wealthy; with Power Prominence,

Or were they rebels, who thrived on, aggression, fear, and dominance?

I still feel, like a kidnapped victim-

Though it's been hundreds of years, there is no Stockholm syndrome.

Will I ever heal from this amnesia, and finally know me?

Probably not; so I curse the lineage of those who stole that from thee,

That someday they know a pain that lies as deep as mine.

If not now, I hope that curse hunts you down next lifetime.

- Timjae A. D'allo

KNOW THYSELF

Not far from the truth, yet equally un-couth

The attire may have changed but the wise recognize the ruse.

From dull colored threads, and whips being clutched,

To tin metal stars, black and white cars, and going so far as to convey that

Justice means "Just Us"

Us being "We", "The People," white like me –

Why is it do you think you are titled minority?

We, the people, a constitution written by all white men,

You; three fifths of a human; where do you think you fit in?

-Oh, white man; only if you knew,

How confused you are; the colored man is you!

Colored; means to change color from its original state,

Well, the creation of my race precedes your sixty five hundred year old birth date.

Hmmm, shall I rouse thee, lest ye be ignorant and lame?

Naw, I think not, food for thought, be gotten by the un-chained.

Signed by the unhanged.

- Timjae A. D'allo

HIGHLY FAVORED

The beautiful thin layer casing my muscles and sinews,

Protects me, yet begets me, banned from many venues.

Though continues to glisten without blister, and smells like CoCoa butter.

But has failed to un-veil unto the pale that walk among us.

The creative designer of ALL things that are, and ever will be –

Fashioned the sun, and therefore melanin to conceal thee,

from degrees of sun burn and skin cancers, to save us.

Would I be wrong, to go on thinking

I, am highly favored!?

My locks, thick and curly, symbolizing **Purity** and **Strength**,

Concentrated! Fore, that which is diluted is flimsy and thin.

Why is it that I win not; in a land of milk and honey?
Fore, it is not; but a land of Fiat Money.

From the land of milk and honey; the "Evil One's" *did* take *us*,

And trade us, for value – I tell you... I...

Am Highly Favored.

– Timjae A. D'allo

EBONY

Sweetness-pure; undiluted Blackamoor; strong, yet nurturing,

Ensnared by her allure.

She's first; with the natural scent of Mother Earth –

Attracted by her nectar,

Though scheming to infect her –

Behold! The Pale White Horse!

Premonition? Could be. Ignorant? We would be, if we choose to ignore

"Signs of the times", a euphemism for caring less,

"Passing the buck"; if you will, on issues we should address.

Declining to digress; I hasten, in this forward Momentum.

Unveiling she, by force! No Choice of ours –

Does he; unable to protect she; make him a coward?

Once, the jewel of a tribe; Guarded, and held on high,

Taken and enslaved; Death could not defeat her.

Mistreating her, gave her fuel; to endure, for the sake of her legacy –

A long tumultuous Journey from whence thou comes;

Still, she is resilient; hopeful; strong;

EBONY

- Timjae A. D'allo

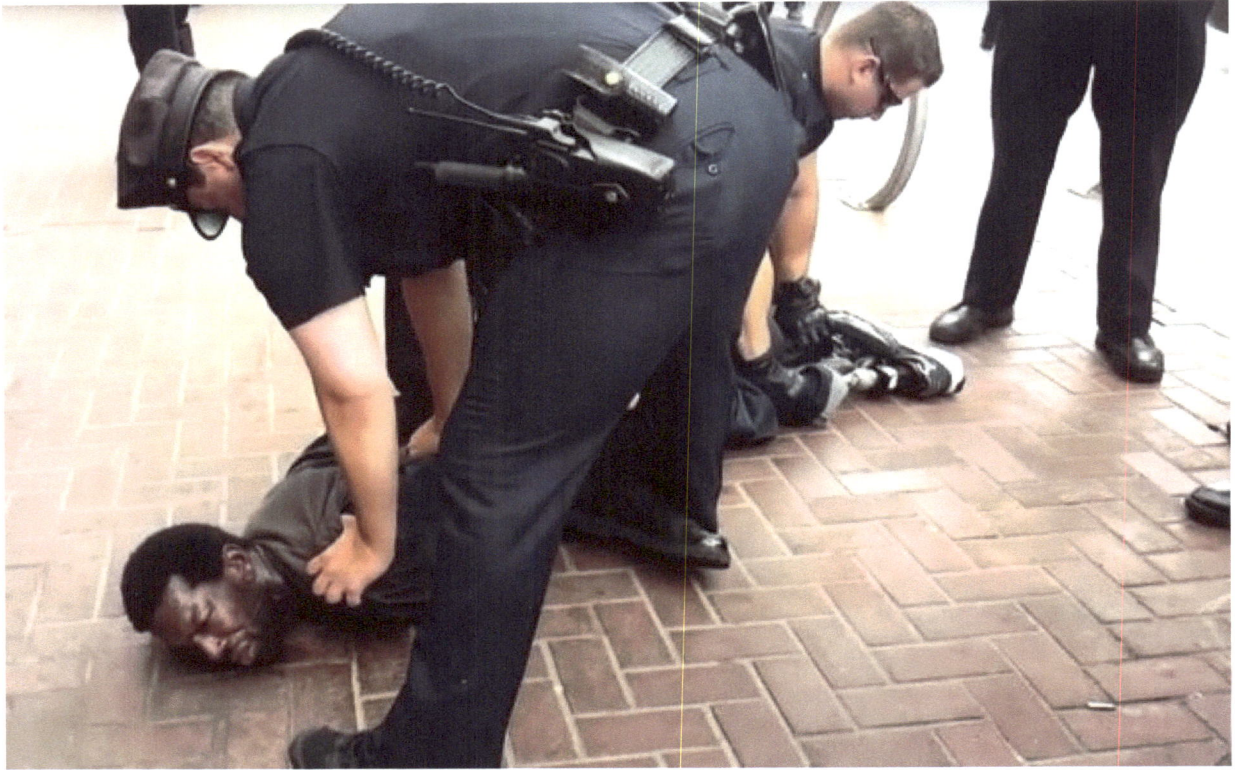

THE BLACK MAN

Abundant vegetation; I shall reap the spoils of my own hands,

With livestock, so I barely shop, but live healthy on my own land.

Still wanna be free; doing best I can, to be my own man.

Provider. Protector. Fighter… Plan to die Standin'.

Live on my knees, not; for me, or generations brought after-

Fore, they will be; bigger, stronger, smarter…. Faster.

Spare my coin; for later days that fail to bring ease,

To feed the 'evil ones' greed, to cure my sick, of his man made disease.

I am awakened! Naïve one, your deeds are not concealed,

As you hover over we, that you killed, even 'till the blood is congealed.

I am the black man

Fill my princess with praise, so that she'll recognize her worth

Raise my young prince on tough love, so he isn't easily hurt.

And my Queen, I'll give her all things, her heart desires on earth

Fore it is She, who hath given me, a Prince, Princess, and her.

I am complete and content. Fearful and repent.

Until my final breath is spent

I am the black man.

- Timjae A. D'allo

I CONTINUE

Intertwined... The Same... Different only in kind.

Of my rib; freely surrendering of oneself to Thine.

Rhythm; Harmonious with mine.

Spiritually obedient in deed, satisfying physical need.

Heed; instructions from above; spill not thy seed.

Lest, ye be punished and lay barren.

Fruitful…. I have made my intentions!

Behold! Ye hath multiplied …. A blessing bestowed

Ye shall know pain…. Cursed; from disobedience past

Trusted; to lead not astray; a child is born.

Of we, to love thee; fore thee are we,

To heir in our wake

Yet, in your blood, bones, and face –

I continue

- Timjae A. D'allo

A STRANGER HERE

I have a back with many lashes; feet blistered by the ashes

From which I remain upright!; withstanding heat and toil,

Suffering;

Yea; the blood boils; Rage, lay coiled –

Yet, even without strike; the river of life stains,

Soiled, the garments of the accused.

Screams of the disparities and tortured goes unheard,

For ye aren't close enough; haven't made it there yet.

To be equals we suggest. Nay; we are equal as equal gets.

Equal gets about three fifths; Declarations of thine captors –

Why is it then, you do not understand, there is only **'nothing'**! That you seek after

When ye **'Arrive'**, be not surprised that **'nothing'** waits inside.

Though suffering, may be for a day; But joy, shall cometh at Sunrise.

Because treasures for thee, will not be stored in this world,

But in a Great Place, and safe space; designed for thine arrival.

After all, I am but a stranger here.

-Timjae A. D'allo

WAIT YOUR TURN

Strong and resilient, you are; know this. But, the world's weight –

Is far too massive to lay flaccid on your plate.

You will not alternate the mandate, when will you recognize?

In their eyes is despise for that betwixt your thighs.

Not because it is oversized; or hers is first prize.

Nay; it is simple multiplication, adding stagnation to your demise.

"Why don't you just die already?" A silent majority exclaims.

Don't get me wrong, not all bare the blame, but if the shoe fits, It's yours.

So behind locked doors, that majority conspires to keep you,

No Conspiracy that '13' is an unlucky number, but for who?

The 13th amendment justifies enslavement and servitude

So let's create Laws;

That are frivolous as; your pants sag to expose your 'draws'

"Let's Lock 'em up!"

Sayeth the Judge in a Convertible, with his mistress wearing next to nothing.

My brotha'; Sit still and be watchful, the Devil has 1,000 years to roam the earth

Fore it is written; and it is ***not*** quittin', if you just simply

Wait your turn

- Timjae A. D'allo

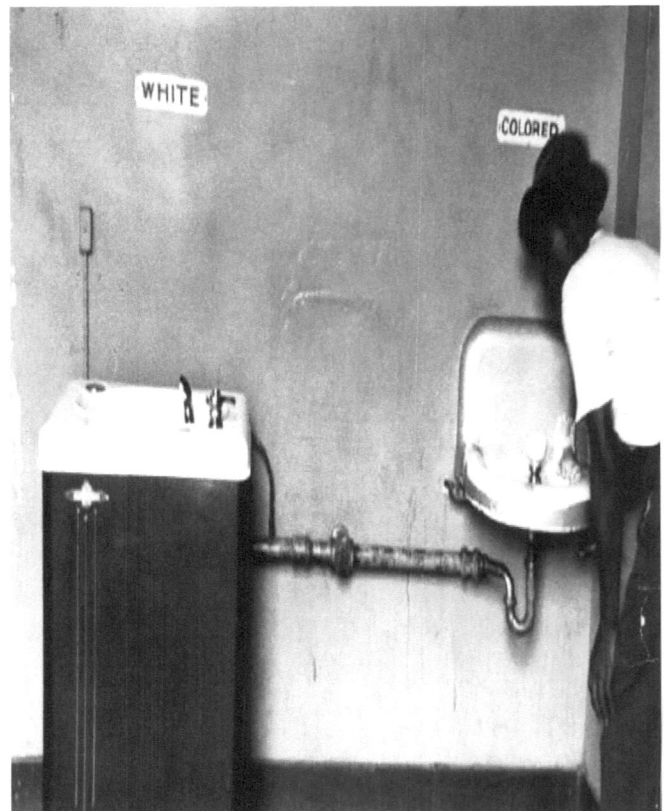

DO YOU REALLY WANT TO KNOW?

The question was posed; why do some call those lacking melanin, Devil?

Well,... let's look into this, and in respect to fairness; keep it level.

What would you call me, if my high pressure firehose banged your frame?

Or if my Shepard's tracked and attacked **you**, like wild game?

What about dubbing you the 'nigger' name,

And claimed that you are less humane –

Extraterrestrial walking among us -

"Make no eye contact with me Nigger! Head to the back of the bus."

And at your stop, when you get thirsty; use that rusty pissed on fountain.

Know your size before you buy, cause no nigger's trying on these outfits.

You can buy my spit on food, but you'll eat it by the out-houses.

And you'll purchase it from the back door,

No eye contact boy, look at the floor!

And this list gets more and more,

But my eyes are misty now, and heart sore.

Do we need to explore more? Do you not see the shame endured?

This is a long line of pain and suffering that has yet to be cured.

Even your history books has skirted the truth, and put on quite a show –

You posed the question; But what I should've asked, was ....

"Do you really want to know? "

RUN

It is my heart that says; Run Brother Run, the Devil will catch you,

You know me not, and still, you hate me – Same Devil, that's you.

That truth, you evade, by the blame of other's deeds?

A black man stole from you, or hit you; but he – is not me.

Shall we, and those like me, also hate you?

A white man, stole from me a lineage, and whipped and hanged me too.

Well, is he also you? Shall you be punished for what he do?

This, is why I run from you. It is never safe to trust it,

We are killed today with no consequence, same as then, when there were muskets.

Run brotha Run! You may get shot in the back –

But fight or flight for your freedom, is reality where we live at.

Mauled by your Shepard's and hounds, scarred by your Tasers,

Captured, chained and bound, then marched before pale faces.

This is what a *slave* gets; but were not talking about a slave yet.

These events are all current, scribed in today's pages.

Four hundred years of oppression, still can't erase this.

Let's face this, 2.2 million; with faces like mine,

Still slaves; says the 13th Amendment in one specific line.

This being sufficient for the blind, to dine –

"Lift yourself up my people," and with this, I Decline,

"They plan to make America Great Again""

-   Run Brotha Run –

-   Timjae A. D'allo

Photograph from Bettmann/Corbis

ITS 2016

Are you sorry for me? Why extend your charities?

Are you guilt ridden, by what was given me, by your family tree?

If you go back far enough, I'm sure you'll see, our family tree's connect...

On your tree, growing however so free, my ancestry hang by their necks.

You say *"It's not like that anymore, its 2016, so let it go,*

It was then, if a slave would run they'd shoot him in the back;

Now, has that changed? No!

See; it is not as clear for you as it is for me.

Just like back then, the evil they wrought, they were too blind to see

You say *"it's not like that anymore, its 2016."* So who's blind?

You or me?

Am I calling you racist? *"No Suh!"*

But, you believe we should know our places,

And by your actions, mine is behind you, 10 to 15 paces

And yeah, its 2016....

- *Timjae A. D'allo*

SPORTS FINAL
DAILY NEWS
FALLEN ANGELS
AMERICA
America's disease
Racist S.C. church shooter captured
GUN VIOLENCE STRIKES NATION AGAIN – PAGES 2,3,4,5,6,7 AND EDITORIAL

TEMPORARY BAN ON MUSLIMS ENTERING U.S.
TRUMP

TIME
BLACK LIVES MATTER.
THIS TIME THE CHARGE IS MURDER

HANDS UP
DONT SHOOT
AUG 9, 2014
R.I.P.
MICHAEL
BROWN

CORRUPTION

We say, *"hallelujah!"* and nine of us are killed by a white man.

We say, *"Asalamu Alaikum!"* and Donald J. Trump declares a muslim ban.

We say, **"Black Lives Matter,"** and it was hardly televised.

White man say's, he'll *"Build a wall"*; It's sensationalized worldwide.

We say, *"You killed an unarmed black teen;"* You say, *"He approached in a threatening manner.*

Yet, a group of **Armed** white men occupy a federal building;

You ignore it, as if it doesn't matter.

We say, *"She wouldn't kill herself over a simple traffic ticket,"*

You say, *"All investigations into this matter has ended."*

We say, *"Affordable health care, has helped our poor and sick heal."*

You say, *"As soon as I'm President, it's the first thing I'll repeal."*

We say, *"There's more blacks incarcerated, than there were slaves in 1865."*

You say, *"Elect me as President, I'll call for longer prison time."*

We say, *"We just wanna be heard"*

You say, were *"Loud and disruptive"*

But we are obviously not loud enough, to end this ***corruption***.

- *Timjae A. D'allo*

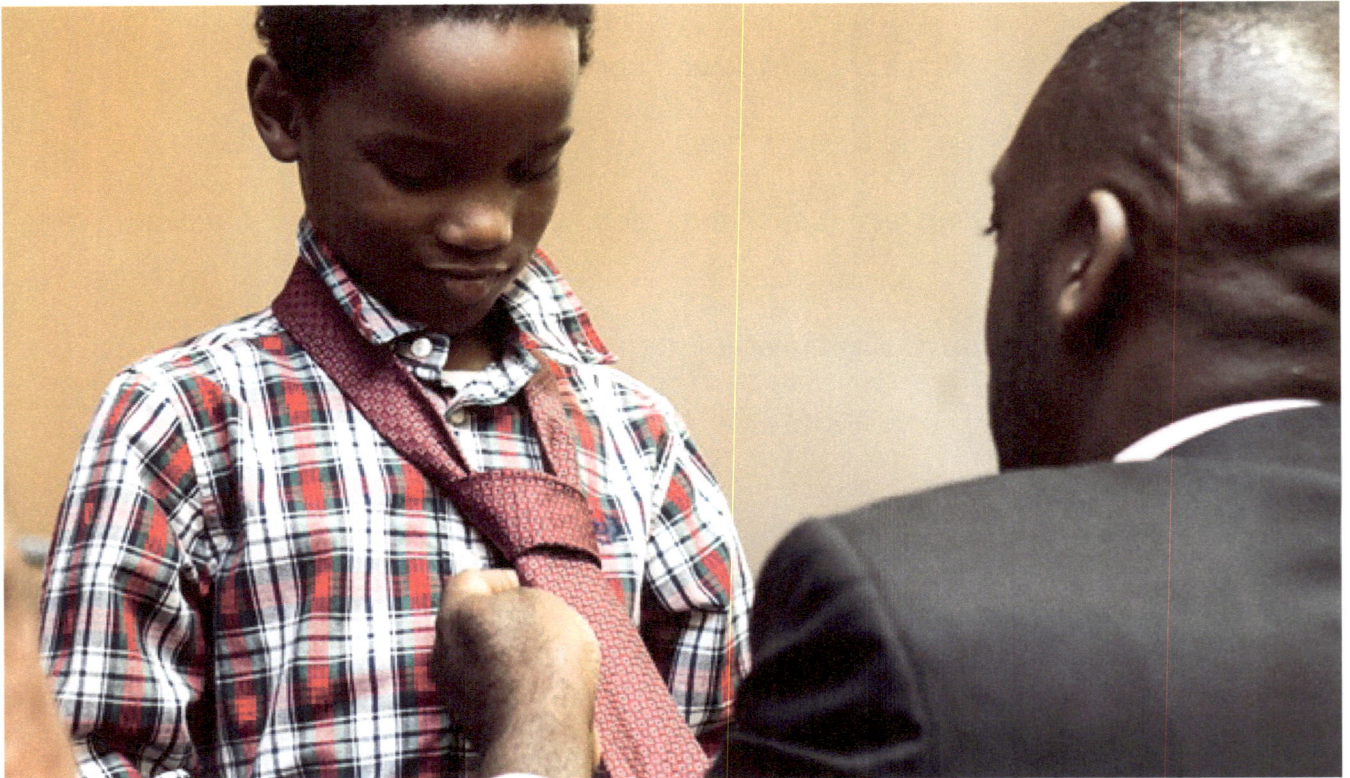

I WONDER

I wonder if white people ever had to say to their child of 7 years young,

"Just because your skin color is different, doesn't mean that you're dumb."

Or, that they have to work twice as hard at succeeding in life, than any other race,

Hmmm? Ever have those confidence building conversations with your child at age 8?

Or asking them to stop saying they hate their dark skin, because it makes them ugly,

And being reassuring when they say "It's because I'm black why they don't trust me."

I wonder….

What is parenting like for the white? Is it a fight, the whole life?

Ever have to put a game face on, and sell to your kids their own life?

Try to pitch it to them, that it's something they'd like if they just give it a try

But deep inside, you know it's gonna really be tough; so does that constitute as a lie?

But; we'll do whatever for our children, right? Some of us even lay down and die,

At least I will; if that's what it takes, for life to deal my children a fair slice of the pie.

Hmmm… I wonder….

-   *Timjae A. D'allo*

A QUEEN

Your brown skin, looks so elegant and demure;

Even your walk and natural Sway of your hips, so graceful and sure.

But he call's you names; and you entertain them

You're a Queen! Order them to be chained, and maim them!

In simpler terms, restrain and abstain from him.

Be ye not content, that you are, as he say you are –

Lest ye be stricken from Queen, to fair maiden tending the barn.

Fore only an animal calls a Queen; whore or bitch,

So refer not to yourself as either, neither, to those you are with.

Recognize, you are a gift, to the soulmate that awaits you –

So, rush not, into the arms of any lost one that will take you.

You could wait, to be guided by the knower of all things,

But you will be guided not; until you first know your

"A Queen"

- *Timjae A. D'allo*

MOMMA… I'M SORRY

With the patience of an oyster; you love me regardless –

But would you love me still, if you knew I'd killed, cause I was heartless?

Or had taken the life of a stranger, that wore a color I didn't like,

Or shot at a crowd of party-goers, for not sending me an invite?

You still see me as your baby…. Said I would always be –

But what you don't know; is everywhere I go, I'm the evil, people see.

Momma…. I'm Sorry.

I embarrassed you, because I brought my gun to church.

But there are people out to get me, so I stay ready to get them first.

And I tricked women into doing things unclean, to boost my wealth –

My moral compass that leads me to love, always led me to myself.

I'm part of a gang that is the same, I even put them before you,

They tell me to kill; you tell me to chill, I do what they tell me to.

Momma…. I'm Sorry.

I'm making amends now. Because at this rate, It won't be long,

Before your putting me in the ground, and crying because I'm gone.

Cry not because I'm gone; But because I couldn't get life straight,

And then smile; because what I did get right; was a final chance to say –

"Momma…. I'm Sorry"

– *Timjae A. D'allo*

‘

I DON'T KNOW

Maybe I should pull my pants up.

And giving up the "N" word would be a nice touch.

Well, hell; if I could quit cursing that would be nice,

Like, calling females bitches – Yup, I know that aint right.

Ooohh, and if I quit drankin' so much, and lay off of the weed;

Yeah, It sounds good …. But could that really be me?

I don't know…

But for sho' I ought to quit sellin' dope,

And maybe quit totin' pistols, before I'm next to get smoked.

What if I retire my flag, and see where that leads;

If I'm not gang bangin' or slangin'; would that really be me?

I don't know….

Man, I should focus on being a Dad, and spend more time with my young –

See what it's like to be a family man; it just might be fun.

But then again, I'm only 21, it's still a lot I want to see –

I think I'd be a pretty hip square, But could that really be me?

I don't now….

But at least, I'm thinking about it.

-   *Timjae A. D'allo*

I'M JUST SAYIN'

Nice cars, shiny jewelry, and expensive clothes –

Adorned by those, who look like we, but see; you've been exposed!

Yeah, you sick! Just like those who tricked us to the slave ships.

We trusted them, but they led us to the 'Evil Ones' as gifts.

Oh, the 'Evil Ones' are slick, time has changed, but not the trick –

Ya see, we are still being led to the 'Evil Ones' as gifts.

They allow in the drugs, and glamorize the drug dealers in movies,

So I try; you catch me, and pack me in a jail like sardines.

Sound familiar? Triple bunked; stacked one nigger atop the other;

If one gets sick, and dies; we throw the body sea-side –

So it's no surprise, prisoners get poor medical care nationwide.

O-yeah, Movie Star, Ball Player, Rapper; you can't hide –

Try some humility; and for the sake of our youth, be careful what you glamorize.

Fore, it is my son, or another one, who will find you to Idolize.

I'm Just Sayin'

-   Timjae A. D'allo

"WHO DO YOU WORK FOR?"

Are you the one who will kill me and consequently, lose your life too?

I'll die now; you'll die in prison, all because I look just like you.

You think were the same, but were not. I'm no killer of any kind,

We may disagree or be enemies; but to kill, is crossing the line.

Who do you work for? … Think about it…. Genocide of the black race,

I bet those overjoyed by your ignorance; were not born with a black face.

Who do you work for, I Say; because they care not how you represent –

Vulgar! In speech and appearance, with drugs pursed between your lips.

A horrible waste of gifts, you were designed to be much greater,

Hit the reset button Quick! And get re-aligned with your creator.

I know what you may be thinking… Say it! I'm sounding something like a hater.

But who do you work for, I say? Because, your sounding something like a traitor!

Hopefully, a seed has been planted, and life will water it for sure,

Unless it has fell on a stony place, and lay bare for the sun to scorch.

But either way; I still wanna know –

"Who do you work for?"

-Timjae A. D'allo

THEY SAY

They Say; "Time heals"….not true; love does

And sometimes, in enough time; we forget what the hurt was.

They say; "as time passes, people begin to lose touch"

Not true; Either the bond was not strong, or the love deep enough.

They say "Time will reveal"… Not true… But life will, In time.

Time is a witness and recorder; so let's pay time no never mind –

We can't alter, or distort it, or figure how much time is left,

They say, "time got away from me" but time only leaves you in death.

If your out of time, your late; ya know; here lies the late John Doe

That's why you shouldn't wait around for people to catch up; Just set your goals and go!

Before you end up late, listening to what "They say"

And just, who in the hell are "they" anyway?

To even care about what they say…. Hhmmmph!!

They say…

- *Timjae A. D'allo*

THE PENITENTIARY

To many, I am so near…. But yet, so far away

I am ever so free…. But against my will, I stay

The sounds around me; disparity, pain, and discontentment

Some even louder; like anger, rage, and resentment.

Sounds that affectively disrupt the atmosphere –

And from where I'm standing; the Sounds I hear, I also see clear.

The silent will not squeak by…. Not here; the silent will be consumed –

By perverted sounds of persuasion, or aggressive ones boomed into a room.

This room is where the sounds of disgust, fear, and death lives

If you don't know, than it's for your own good you don't recognize where, "this" is.

I hear Dead People!! Coming and going non-stop –

Better keep their sounds out of my bubble, I'm walking Dead trouble

Head Shot!!

-   *Timjae A. D'allo*

SINCERELY-

Dear Racist, there is a few things I'd like to say;

First of all, I did not kidnap you and make you slaves.

Nor, did I strip you nude, to buy, sell, or trade.

Nor did I forcibly rape your women to breed a lighter grade.

I surely didn't cut into your back with whips, like a blade –

Or take you out back and shoot you, for trying to run away.

And when you were freed; I didn't work you for chitterling pay,

Neither did I hang, mutilate, or burn you; for looking my woman's way.

I definitely didn't spray my fire hose; or have dog's bite you in the face

Of course, I never burned any of your churches; just to spite God's Grace –

And you know, I never asked for your vote, while I advocate hate, during my

Presidential Campaign Race....

So what gives? Why do you hate me so? And I don't hate you –

Is this a tantrum for having no one else to torture, or to be your footstool?

I call you Devil; not because I hate you; But because your evil to the core,

And after all these things I never done to you; your still bitter and sore.

P.S.

Why do you hate me so? Do you even know? Is it because were fighting to be equal?

Ah, forget it; I'll pray for you, is what I'm gonna do;

Sincerely,

Black People

- Timjae A. D'allo

ABOUT THE AUTHOR

Timjae Arihan D'Allo is a Muslim American and Black Man unapologetically. He is from Oakland, CA and a proud husband and father, driven to make change in this world one paragraph at a time.